KENYA

Big Buddy Books
An Imprint of Abdo Publishing
abdopublishing.com

Julie Murray

abdopublishing.com

Published by Abdo Publishing, a division of ABDO, PO Box 398166, Minneapolis, Minnesota 55439.
Copyright © 2018 by Abdo Consulting Group, Inc. International copyrights reserved in all countries. No part
of this book may be reproduced in any form without written permission from the publisher. Big Buddy Books™
is a trademark and logo of Abdo Publishing.

Printed in the United States of America, North Mankato, Minnesota.
052017
092017

THIS BOOK CONTAINS
RECYCLED MATERIALS

Cover Photo: ©iStockphoto.com.
Interior Photos: ASSOCIATED PRESS (p. 17); Stuart Boulton/Alamy Stock Photo (p. 35); dbimages/Alamy
Stock Photo (p. 5); Images of Africa Photobank/Alamy Stock Photo (pp. 25, 35); ©iStockphoto.com
(pp. 9, 11, 13, 15, 21, 23, 27, 34, 35, 37); John Warburton-Lee Photography/Alamy Stock Photo (p. 11);
Marion Kaplan/Alamy Stock Photo (p. 13); REUTERS/Alamy Stock Photo (p. 19); John Shearer/Invision/
AP (p. 31); Shutterstock.com (pp. 23, 38); Sipa USA via AP (p. 33); Steve Taylor ARPS/Alamy Stock
Photo (p. 29); Ariadne Van Zandbergen/Alamy Stock Photo (p. 16).

Coordinating Series Editor: Tamara L. Britton
Editor: Katie Lajiness
Graphic Design: Taylor Higgins, Keely McKernan

Country population and area figures taken from the CIA World Factbook.

Publisher's Cataloging-in-Publication Data

Names: Murray, Julie, 1969- , author.
Title: Kenya / by Julie Murray.
Description: Minneapolis, MN : Abdo Publishing, 2018. | Series: Explore the
    countries | Includes bibliographical references and index.
Identifiers: LCCN 2016962350 | ISBN 9781532110498 (lib. bdg.) |
    ISBN 9781680788341 (ebook)
Subjects: LCSH: Kenya--Juvenile literature.
Classification: DDC 967.62--dc23
LC record available at http://lccn.loc.gov/2016962350

KENYA

CONTENTS

Around the World

Our world has many countries. Each country has beautiful land. It has its own rich history. And, the people have their own languages and ways of life.

Kenya is a country in Africa. What do you know about Kenya? Let's learn more about this place and its story!

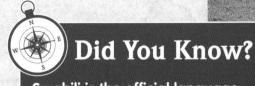

Did You Know?

Swahili is the official language in Kenya.

The Nyayo Monument is in Uhuru Park in Nairobi. This monument honors President Daniel arap Moi who ruled from 1978 to 2002.

SAY IT

Kenya
KEH-nyuh

PASSPORT TO KENYA

Kenya is on the eastern coast of Africa. It shares borders with five countries. The Indian Ocean is to the east.

The country's total area is about 224,081 square miles (580,367 sq km). Nearly 47 million people live there.

Did You Know?

Kenya is more than twice the size of Nevada.

WHERE IN THE WORLD?

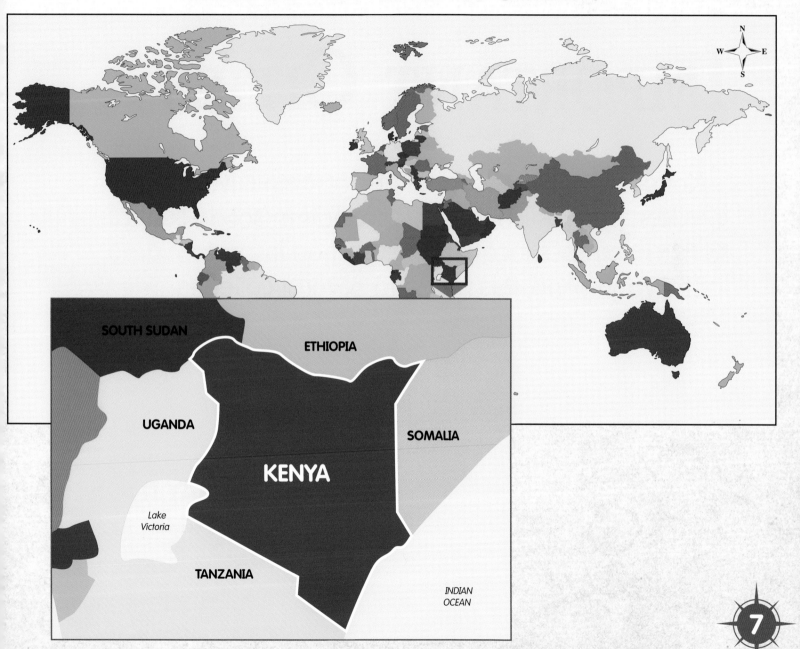

IMPORTANT CITIES

Nairobi is Kenya's **capital** and largest city. Nearly 4 million people live there. The city is in south-central Kenya. Nairobi's location makes it an important area for railways. And, it is home to several colleges.

SAY IT
Nairobi
neye-ROH-bee

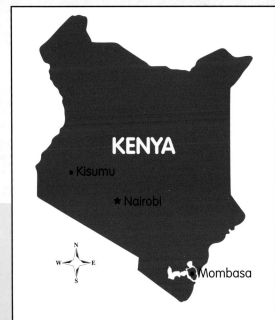

KENYA

• Kisumu

★ Nairobi

Mombasa

Nairobi National Park is just outside the city's downtown area. This park is home to more than 400 different kinds of animals such as giraffes.

Mombasa is Kenya's second-largest city. More than 1 million people live there. It is an island in the Indian Ocean. Throughout history, Mombasa has been fought over and ruled by different groups. Today, the city is Kenya's main port.

Kisumu is Kenya's third-largest city. More than 390,000 people live there. Kisumu is on the shores of Lake Victoria. Until the 1970s, the local port was active and provided many jobs. Today, the main businesses are farming and manufacturing clothes.

A ferry connects Mombasa to mainland Kenya. More than 300,000 people ride the ferry every day.

SAY IT

Mombasa
mahm-BAH-suh

Kisumu
kee-SOO-moo

Lake Victoria in Kisumu borders Tanzania and Uganda. It is the largest freshwater lake in Africa.

Kenya in History

One of the world's earliest **cultures** began in what is now Kenya. For thousands of years, Africans traded with **Arabs** from across the Indian Ocean. In the 1800s, the British took over Kenya. It became a British colony in 1920.

In 1952, Kenyans fought the British. Kenya wanted independence. A group known as the Mau Mau led the fight against Britain. In 1963, Kenya won its freedom. The next year, Kenya elected its first president.

Kenyatta International Conference Center is in Nairobi. Built in 1974, it is 345 feet (105 m) tall and has 32 floors.

Jomo Kenyatta was Kenya's first president. He served from 1964 until his death in 1978.

For decades, Kenya fought for its **democracy**. In 1982, Kenya's president made his political party the only legal party. It wasn't until 1991 that other parties could join in elections.

In 2011, East Africa suffered its worst **drought** in 60 years. The lack of rain caused problems for 13 million people in Kenya, Ethiopia, and Somalia. Aid groups brought relief through food, water, and health care.

At one time, Dadaab was the world's largest refugee camp. More than 326,000 people from other countries lived there. It is set to close in 2017.

TIMELINE

About 3.3 million BC

The earliest humans began using tools in what is now Kenya.

AD 600

Arabs settled coastal areas and developed trading stations.

1498

The Vasco Da Gama Pillar was built on Kenya's coast. It is the oldest monument in Africa.

1982

The country's National Assembly allowed only one political party.

2012

Oil was discovered in Kenya.

2015

Barack Obama made his first visit to Kenya as US president. His father was born there.

An Important Symbol

Kenya's flag has three stripes. They are black, red, and green. In the center, a shield and two spears stand for **defending** freedom.

Kenya is a **republic**. The president is the head of government. The president serves a five-year term.

In 2010, Kenya adopted a new **constitution**. It included a bill of rights to help protect all Kenyans.

Kenya's flag was adopted in 1963.

SAY IT

Uhuru Kenyatta
OO-huhr-roo KEHN-yah-tah

In 2013, Uhuru Kenyatta was elected as Kenya's president. He is the country's fourth president and the son of Kenya's first president.

ACROSS THE LAND

Kenya has deserts, mountains, plains, rivers, and valleys. Kenya's most important river is the Tana. It runs 440 miles (708 km) and flows from the Aberdare Mountains to the Indian Ocean.

The highest peak in Kenya is Mount Kenya. It is 17,057 feet (5,199 m) high. Mount Kenya is the second-highest peak in Africa.

Mount Kilimanjaro is the highest mountain in Africa. While the mountain is in Tanzania, it can be seen from Amboseli National Park in Kenya.

Did You Know?

In Kenya, the average temperature is 85°F (16°C).

Evergreen forests and bamboo grow in Kenya's highlands. Low trees grow east and west of the highlands. In the north, thorn bushes are common.

Several types of animals live in Kenya. They include elephants, leopards, lions, and zebras. Many of these animals live in national parks and on wildlife preserves.

Lions live on the Masai Mara National Reserve in Kenya. People visit the reserve to see lions in the wild.

Acacia trees grow in Kenya. They produce a gum used in many products such as glues and drugs.

Earning a Living

Kenya produces a lot of important goods. Most Kenyans are farmers. They grow coffee, corn, flowers, and tea. Factory workers make products such as cloth, flour, paper, and sugar.

Many people work in the service industry. Travelers come from around the world to go on **safari** in Kenya. Visitors get to see animals up close in the wild.

In Kenya, farmers place coffee beans on drying trays. The beans cannot be processed until they are dry.

LIFE IN KENYA

Kenya has a rich **cultural** history. Over time, different types of people came to Kenya. They brought their own arts, foods, and hobbies.

Kenyans are known for their woodcarvings. These carvings are often of animals or people. They are also known for their beadwork. Bracelets and necklaces are the most popular beaded pieces.

In Kenya, every community has its own native food. Common foods in Kenya include kale, rice, and spinach. Meat is only eaten in small amounts or on special occasions.

Maasai women wear traditional beadwork as part of their culture.

Kenyans love to play and watch soccer. Basketball, netball, and volleyball are also popular throughout the country.

Faith is an important part of life in Kenya. Most people are **Christians.** Smaller groups follow **Islam** or traditional African religions.

Did You Know?

In Kenya, students must attend school from ages 6 to 14. All students can attend school for free.

Netball is similar to basketball. However, there is no dribbling or running with the ball. More than 20 million people around the world play netball.

29

Famous Faces

Many talented people are from Kenya. Lupita Nyong'o was born on March 1, 1983, in Mexico City, Mexico. Her parents are from Kenya. The family moved back to Kenya when she was a child.

Nyong'o came to the United States to study filmmaking and acting. Her first role after graduation was in the film *12 Years a Slave*. For this role, she won an **Academy Award** for Best Supporting Actress.

SAY IT

Lupita Nyong'o
loo-PEE-tah n-YAWNG-o

Nyong'o is the first Kenyan actress to win an Academy Award.

Eliud Kipchoge is a world-class runner. He was born on November 5, 1984, in Kapsisiywa, Kenya.

In 2003, Kipchoge won the 5,000-meter race at the world championships in Paris, France. A year later, he won a bronze medal at the Olympics in the same event.

In 2013, Kipchoge ran and won his first marathon! At the 2016 Olympics in Rio de Janeiro, Brazil, he won gold in the marathon. He ran 26.2 miles (42 km) with a time of 2:08:44.

SAY IT

Eliud Kipchoge
El-ee-yood kip-CHOH-gay

During the 2016 Olympics, Kipchoge won by one more than one minute.

TOUR BOOK

Imagine traveling to Kenya! Here are some places you could go and things you could do.

 **Climb**

Near Mount Kenya, the sun rises and sets at the same time every day.

 **Relax**

Diani Beach is part of a large resort. Visitors love to swim in the clear water and then sit under a palm tree.

 Explore

Masai Mara National Reserve takes you on **safari**. See wildebeest as they travel to find food.

 See

Jambo Kenya Deluxe is a train that goes from Nairobi to Mombasa. It passes through beautiful landscapes.

Learn

The Menengai Crater is a dead volcano in Nakuru, Kenya. Bike or hike near the crater and enjoy the view of Lake Nakuru.

A GREAT COUNTRY

The story of Kenya is important to our world. Kenya is a land of wild animals and breathtaking landscapes. It is a country of people who love their country.

The people and places that make up Kenya offer something special. They help make the world a more beautiful, interesting place.

At Lake Nakuru National Park, the land and animals are protected from harm.

Kenya Up Close

Official Name: Republic of Kenya

Flag:

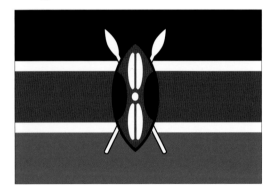

Population (rank): 46,790,758
(July 2016 est.)
(31st most-populated country)

Total Area (rank): 224,081 square miles (49th
Largest country)

Capital: Nairobi

Official Languages: Swahili and English

Currency: Kenyan shillings

Form of Government: Republic

National Anthem: "Ee Mungu Nguvu Yetu"
("Oh God of All Creation")

IMPORTANT WORDS

Academy Award an award given by the Academy of Motion Picture Arts and Sciences to the best actors and filmmakers of the year.

Arab a member of the people who are originally from the Arabian Peninsula and who now live mostly in the Middle East and northern Africa.

capital a city where government leaders meet.

Christian (KRIHS-chuhn) a person who practices Christianity, which is a religion that follows the teachings of Jesus Christ.

constitution (kahnt-stuh-TOO-shuhn) the basic laws that govern a country or a state.

culture (KUHL-chuhr) the arts, beliefs, and ways of life of a group of people.

defend to fight danger in order to keep safe.

democracy a governmental system in which the people vote on how to run their country.

drought (DRAUT) a long period of dry weather.

Islam a religion based on a belief in Allah as God and Muhammad as his prophet.

republic a government in which the people choose the leader.

safari a journey to see or hunt animals, especially in Africa.

WEBSITES

To learn more about Explore the Countries, visit **abdobooklinks.com**. These links are routinely monitored and updated to provide the most current information available.

INDEX